...ries Boyle was born in Leeds in 1951. He has taught English in the UK and abroad, and now works in publishing. He lives in London.

by the same author

SLEEPING ROUGH
THE VERY MAN
PALEFACE

CHARLES BOYLE

The Age of
Cardboard and String

———

faber and faber

First published in 2001
by Faber and Faber Limited
3 Queen Square London WC1N 3AU
Published in the United States by Faber and Faber, Inc.,
an affiliate of Farrar, Straus and Giroux, New York

Photoset by Wilmaset Ltd, Birkenhead, Wirral
Printed in England by
MPG Books Limited, Victoria Square, Bodmin, Cornwall

The right of Charles Boyle to be identified as author
of this work has been asserted in accordance with Section 77
of the Copyright, Designs and Patents Act 1988

A CIP record for this book
is available from the British Library

ISBN 0-571-20667-0

ACKNOWLEDGEMENTS

Some of these poems were first printed in: *The Guardian, Last Words*
(Picador, 1999), *London Magazine, Poetry Review, Poetry Wales, Stand,
Thumbscrew, Times Literary Supplement.*

The author thanks The Authors' Foundation for financial support
during the summer of 1998.

2 4 6 8 10 9 7 5 3 1

for Toby and Lucian,
and for Madeleine

Contents

PART THREE

'What!' cried the Duchess in amazement. 'It is you, sir, who are one of the greatest poets of this age, the famous Ferrante Palla?'

'Famous, maybe, but most unfortunate, that is certain.'

'And a man of your talent, sir, is obliged to steal in order to live?'

'That, perhaps, is the reason why I have some talent.'

Stendhal, *La Chartreuse de Parme*, Chapter 21

"...had given the Duchess to understand ... free you are who
are one of the greatest poets of the age, the King, or perhaps
Pallas."

"Famous, yes ... but most unfortunate ... that is remand
And an ... of your ... childs ... to ... its ... "

"That perhaps is the ... who blame your ..."

wonderful. As between a ... Poet & Clippers ...

PART ONE

A Respectable Neighbourhood

I was walking with irregular strides, avoiding
the cracks in the pavement and keeping a weather eye open
for the humdrum but telling detail –
the one I could never make up,
the proof that I tell no lie –
when this woman starts screaming blue murder
from an upper window. *Fuck you!*
she was yelling, and meaning it, and only stopped
to draw breath when I came to a stop myself.

A black-haired beauty, souls
have been sold for less.
I was flattered but about to move on
when she threw down a blue checked shirt –
followed by, in random order, pants,
jeans, a jumper and scuffed leather jacket,
half a dozen compact discs
and a copy of *La Chartreuse de Parme*
that, when it hit the ground, fell open
at chapter twenty-one, 'A Strange Encounter'.

The window slammed shut.
The sun ducked behind a bank of clouds.
A man dressed too smartly for comfort
stepped out of the doorway and gave me a look
that implied I should make myself scarce.

Will Fabrizio escape from the citadel?
Will Clelia cheat on her vow

never to set eyes on him again?
As I bent to retrieve the book
I felt like a thief of dead men's boots
on the field at Waterloo.

Hotel Rosa

In the open briefcase
of the man across the aisle
on the bus from the airport
lies the manuscript of my poems.

I keep sneaking glances,
wondering about that haircut.

As we cross the lagoon,
and a smell of decaying fish
pervades the bus,
he turns to face me
with the look of one interrupted
by yet another of the pointless
bureaucratic intrusions
to which travellers are prone.

*

The style, Herr Fischer remarks of A—,
over our breakfast omelette
under the jacaranda tree
at the Hotel Rosa,
is that of a man
whose work has been translated
into forty-two languages
and then back into English.

His fingers are long and bony
but heavy on the keys.

From his room overlooking the garden
bouts of regular typing
alternate with curious bleats.

*

Two lime-green Sunbeam taxis
idle outside the gate.
One driver is asleep,
the other reminds me
of a tennis ex-pro
my father once packed me off to
after school, to practise my backhand.

I can't write a thing ...
Herr Fischer has asked me
for a list of my favourite songs.

*

Sleep deprivation
may account for my headache today.
Last night, as we sat on the verandah
counting the fireflies,
an almighty splashing –
then a tall red-bearded man
came stumbling towards us,
shaking water off his clothes
like a wet dog.

Lawrence has arrived
with his difficult wife.

*

The Lawrences, Herr Fischer and I
shared a taxi to the open-air museum.

'The working model
of the funicular railway
(the original having been damaged
beyond repair) was made
by the metalwork class
of the boys' reformatory...'

Somehow I lost the others
and then got lost myself.
I am writing this
in a bar near the harbour,
surrounded by naked women
and drunken Chinese sailors.
Rarely have I been so happy.

*

Herr Fischer's birthday.
A storm that came out of nowhere
has cut off the electricity.
We play cards by candlelight
with the hotel proprietor,
who lost an arm in the war
(*Which* war? I keep meaning to ask.)

In the yard at the back for cars
Lawrence is attempting to light a fire
of unseasoned wood
to spit-roast a kid.

Rain at the window again ...
I feel certain that Frieda is cheating.

*

Lawrence at a loss for words!
Going down to the lobby
to ask for a plug for the bath,
I find him failing to convince
an itinerant vendor
of the worth of his Seiko watch.

He seems none too sure himself
of the provenance
of the mahogany statuette he desires.

*

Is it something I said?
Herr Fischer is avoiding me.
All day I've been carrying around
the money I owe him
from our game of pontoon.

*

So quiet this morning.
Alone in the dining room,
I very gently banged the gong.
There followed a shriek of laughter
from behind the kitchen door.

Herr Fischer and Lawrence
have departed upriver

on the trail of dark gods,
leaving me to cope as I can
with poor Frieda.

An Earring

We rang for room service and the year 1913 answered.
Velimir Khlebnikov

Would it help if I opened the window?
Polished my shoes?
Put on some music and slowly undressed you?

– You, at the end of your tether, searching for an earring
that cannot not be in this room;
me, thinking along the lines above,
when it strikes me that the traffic outside
is moving unnaturally slowly,
is stuck in fact in that silent slow motion
with which events are perceived to unfold
before an imminent and unavoidable catastrophe,
as if they already belong to a bygone era.

Follain's Leeds

Dead men walk down Briggate,
men killed by heavy machinery,
in boating accidents,
by diseases of body or mind.

Men killed on the Somme,
their faces chewed by rats,
stroll down Briggate
with all the time in the world.

One enters a barber's shop
and takes his place before a mirror
in which, behind him, a boy can be glimpsed
sweeping the hairs on the floor.

Seven Poems from Prose by Stendhal

The War Office

At the end of the garden were some unfortunate, heavily pruned lime-trees, behind which we used to go to pee. They were the first friends that I had in Paris.

Stendhal, La Vie de Henry Brulard

I watched my pee soak into the soil –
so quickly, so eagerly did the trees drink it up,
no one, it seemed, had loved them as I.

My fingers were black
from the writing of letters – to this or that
quartermaster, to absconding paymasters,
kindly requesting ... I too,
I said to myself, will one day wax my moustache,
sprout epaulettes, take an Italian opera singer
for my mistress – we will send the hussars north,
the dragoons south, campaign medals
will be struck.

       Piqued
by my lack of attention, my friends
would become agitated, shaking leaves and birds
from their stunted branches
and setting up a wind
that travelled, for all I know, as far as Grenoble.

Gradually, reluctantly even,
they grew quiet and still, wondering
at their own strength.

Crossing the Saint-Bernard

During our evening halts he began to pass on to me some of the
principles of swordsmanship. 'Otherwise you'll get yourself
skewered like a ...' I've forgotten the term of comparison.
                    Stendhal, La Vie de Henry Brulard

> *La gloire* of the sunsets!
> Our blades flashing
> in the high mountain air!
> Clouds drenched in the colour –
> it comes back to me now –
> of ice in the gutter
> outside the slaughterhouse.

In the Town of X

When I arrive in a town I always ask: 1. Who are the twelve prettiest women? 2. Who are the twelve richest men? 3. Which man could have me hanged?

Stendhal, *Souvenirs d'Egotisme*

The apprentice stylist, wiping the mirrors
in the empty salon,
then inspecting her gums;

the sisters in the orchard;
their seasoned mother; the outspoken
librarian, biting her lip through the day;

the homesick exchange student,
her reddened eyes and perfect shrug;
the miscast Lady Macbeth,
chain-smoking in the green room;

the cardinal's daughter;
the dental hygienist with flu;
the undertaker's widow;

and the woman in Zeno's pâtisserie
like the woman in that painting by Manet
behind the bar, bored
by the whiskers and paintbrushes of men –

little shivers of happiness
as one by one each places her hand
on the bevel of my hip,

while the chief of police
and eleven other rich men
jangling their keys, ordering more brandy,
avert their eyes.

*

Rainy afternoons,
we trail through the furniture emporium:
so much chrome, veneer and lacquer
gives us a headache, we want to lie down ...

Or we take in a matinee at the temperance hall
by The Man Who Has All The Answers:
patient and exact, he fields every question
as if no one has asked it before.

The sky afterwards is overwhelmingly bright –
like matrimony, like just having bought something
you've saved up for for years,
or a stage-set for an execution.

Sunday

Ah, it's Sunday, I say to myself. Instantly any inner tendency
towards happiness vanishes.

Stendhal, *La Vie de Henry Brulard*

Leeds win away, and a man outside the newsagent's
mumbling *Merry Christmas! Merry Christmas!*

though it's already early March,
and they've left it too late for a place in Europe.

I hunker back to bed
to lick my belovèd's nipples

while she reads aloud from 'The Work of Art
in the Age of Mechanical Reproduction'.

[17]

The Picnic

He was a very handsome young man, and spent his whole life in the woods with a hammer in his hand.

Stendhal, *La Chartreuse de Parme*

I lay down in the grass, replete.
Naked women flitted in and out of the trees.

Next time I looked, bandits with antique rifles
were creeping towards me.

*

Though my heart was beating
like the *tap-tap-tap*
of a tiny hammer, I remained quite calm.

They had not been bandits long
and had wives and children to support
and were lousy shots –

even when a rabbit
took pity, and made itself
a sitting target, they missed.

*

Pedro was wounded. I tied the picnic rug
to two branches, and dragged him into the shade.

He told me about his childhood sweetheart
to whom he sent letters in code
that were intercepted.

About the bullets fired into the air
at weddings, and about the naked women.

*

Never to be alone again
among the apple cores and beakers
with a wind getting up, raising the paper napkins
like flags of surrender ...

*

I wrote down his last wish
and buried it under a stone.

Rainy Days

We were in the country, it was pouring with rain, and we were only too happy to listen to her.

Stendhal, *De l'amour*

Dogs stop padding about, children
fretting, even the servants
replacing buckets
under the leaking gallery roof
become rapt, becalmed.

Soup is brought in,
lobster bisque. Blankets,
logs. I make furtive exits
to shake off my pins and needles,
to see to the horses,
to check the closing prices ...

By the third day
the water is up to our ankles.
On the sixth, the abbé's bloated,
drifting corpse
becomes snagged on the piano stool.

Is she making this up, I wonder,
as she goes along?
Sometimes I turn the volume right down,
watch her mouth sweet nothings –

like rain on the sea,
or the continuous wavering *shhhhh*
of traffic on the motorway
across two fields.

The Disguise

*During the crossing it occurred to me that by wearing green
spectacles and changing my coat I could quite well spend two or
three days at Volterra, going out only at night and without being
recognised by you.*
        Stendhal, letter to Matilde Dembowski, 11 June 1819

So that you wouldn't know I was following you,
I wore a second-hand coat and green sunglasses.
I arrived on the 3rd. It was open day
at the asylum, madmen were out on the streets
canvassing for the ruling party. A plush hotel
rented rooms by the hour; in the lobby, secret policemen
posed as gypsies selling lucky charms.
Priests were suspicious, bank managers friendly:
I seemed young and single and on the make.
I entered a café where others of my kind
were gathered in disguise: an eye patch or glass eye,
a toupée or false moustache. Women too,
smoking cigars. (So that no one might know I loved you,
I never spoke your name. So that no one might know
you did not love me back, I became a wit, a raconteur,
a boulevardier.) We debated pre-Columbian art,
heatedly. The pots in the archaeological institute
are fakes, every one of them, even the shards.
The real ones are kept in the livery stables,
packed in dry manure. The town was a hothouse,
though the sky was grey. I was so lathered in sweat

I couldn't sleep. I gave my coat to a beggar
outside the Selci Gate, a veteran of the Somme.
I took off my glasses. I had everything to lose.

My Alibi

I had gone to meet my love
in a bar behind the abbey. A damp
November night, darkness
thickening, and a cold mist
spreading from the river through the narrow streets
of tearooms, giftshops and, I supposed,
superior brothels. Patient
as an animal, a horse or guide-dog, a single taxi
waited outside a mullioned door,
its engine breathing softly,
and a tourist both lost and drunk asked me directions
to the nearest underground.

I was standing in front of the backlit window
of a religious bookshop, studying
the edifying titles, when a clock chimed,
I didn't count, and then again
much later, and when at last, in an alley
I must have passed and repassed, I found the bar,
my love had gone. Three angels
playing cards at a corner table
beckoned me over, and we debated
until dawn the fine distinctions
between the sacred and profane, between the essence
and the energies of God.

The Nature Trail

You with your sensible shoes
         and your dog on a lead,
turn a blind eye
         to the tell-tale remains
of a fire, the empty
         half-bottle of vodka,
and don't disturb
         the rowing boat
stuck fast among the reeds,
         the *Lady Blue*,
I may need it soon
         to scarper downriver.

PART TWO

Life Class

A wind comes and goes, failing to attach itself.
Just two or three smokers, the last Mohicans
at their fire-eating ritual
on the steps of the adult education institute,
while upstairs in the life room the model
of hardly classical proportions,
his chubby penis at rest between his thighs,
silently recites the *Idylls of the King*
to the mid-morning class of retired postmen, housewives
and Scandinavian au pairs.

                   From the upper floors
of the neurological hospital, stuntmen sway out
with their kit for washing windows. A parked
Sierra is leaking brake fluid, a blue Mercedes
stalking a space. And Merlin in a suit
stands in a flowerbed to issue his prophecy
on a mobile phone: that challenged to bare her soul,
a girl today will up-end her shoulder bag
and spill out among the ruins of lunch
cough sweets, comb, bus pass, address book, loose change
and a lizard –
            green, the span of your hand,
eyeing both sides equally, and but for a flick
or a blink, already a part of the décor.

Hosea: A Commentary

Reaping a whirlwind, I remarked, pointing to the words on the sandwich board that was leaning against his chair as he sipped his cappuccino: a bit steep for a spot of adultery between consenting adults? He said he didn't think it was meant literally, it was more a figure of speech, and I warmed to him at once – not at all the uptight evangelical type I'd expected, the sort with metal fatigue who could crack open at any moment and spill their payload across the hinterland of a major industrial city. So the palaces devoured by fire, the slaying of the fruit of the womb, the infants dashed in pieces... ? He said he couldn't be one hundred per cent sure – he was only doing this job while Hosea was away on vacation, he had a place at college to read immunology in September – but basically, at the root of it all, the issue was pollution. We let the word rest between us for a while, it had the right anthropological ring, until we noticed a man walking past in sandals, muttering to himself through his long grey beard. I could feel my boy becoming a bit edgy – that was Isaiah himself, and the prophets were supposed to stick to their own streets, there was a gentleman's agreement. Luckily a hairdresser's over the road was still open, a few late customers were sitting on leather sofas reading up the tips on foreplay in glossy magazines. We each took one of Isaiah's arms and hustled him in for a haircut. He offered only token resistance, I think secretly he was quite happy.

Second Alibi (Other Business)

I was wearing a suit,
a little loose around the shoulders,
a little tight around the waist ...

Item four: the budget cuts.
The chairman stripped off his jacket
and rolled up his sleeves,
meaning business.

Item fifteen: staffing levels.
Item forty-nine: storage retrieval ...

By the small hours, the ones
that seem so long, the ones that remind you
of a chart on the classroom wall
explaining evolution, he had fallen asleep
over the lingerie ads
in the company report.

We were wondering about the boy
we'd sent out for sandwiches
when my father stepped into the frame
in his pinstripe, patting his inside pockets.

He had lost his wallet
or was making the sign of the cross.
I was doodling an infinite system
of interlocking pagodas.

Railway Porters

Their sad, all-weather composure, subdued
livery, their intimate knowledge of weights
and Yorkshire cricket – as you unlocked the car
and ruffled my hair
and fumbled in your pocket for loose change.

Inside the boot of every Riley,
inside a leather case inside a leather case
is my father's monogrammed set of ivory brushes.

The Age of Cardboard and String

It is a machine for eating oranges.
It is a machine for humming new tunes.
It is a rocket bound for the moon.
It is, whichever string you pull, the same machine.

When it breaks we apply more sellotape,
and when it breaks again we sulk, mixing our tears
into the glue. When it works

we set off for the moon,
scattering orange peel on the floor
and singing songs not yet written down –
hot, fierce songs

that almost burn our mouths with their newness.

*

Faster! Faster! We want to overtake
Anna, who is seven. We want

gears, automatic transmission, wings, clouds
to fly through, flags, fuel injection,
solar panels, stabilisers, sometimes just
to be left alone.

And no,
it wasn't us (with crumbs on our lips)
who stole the cookies from the cookie jar.

Maybe God.
Maybe God was hungry.

※

The moon was OK.
There were holes in it,
we saw biscuits and things at the bottom.

It was raining, the cardboard melted.
Tomorrow can we build a boat?

Wait! We brought you back a secret,
but we're going to tell it to the zebras first –
the black one with stripes painted white,
the white one with stripes painted black,

who sleep on the landing,
leaving just enough room to squeeze by.

Things to Do Indoors

when it's raining, for example, or you are waiting
for your lover to arrive, or a curfew
is in force. Make a clock that runs backwards
with an alarm that is timed to go off
at the moment of your birth, and so wake you up
to your before-life. The recent years
will be familiar, so cut a life-size silhouette
of your head and upper body from stiff black card
and tape it to the window – there, now you are free
to hurry out to the shops for more wine,
more cigarettes, forgetting to switch on the answerphone
before you leave. Drink the wine from one of a pair
of Venetian goblets; smash the other against a wall
for luck. Fall asleep on the sofa
and dream you are Isadora Duncan
driving her bright red sports car on the Riviera
at tremendous speed: the road is narrow,
there are many hairpin bends, the sea to your left
glitters like sequins, like the several million beating wings
of a plague of locusts heading inland. Place just one
under your microscope, invented in circa 1650
by Antoni von Leeuwenhoek. The Dutch
of that time, both housewives and painters,
preferred their interiors spick and span, bathed
by the cool clear light that follows rain.

The Break

My brother was nicknamed hedgehog at school
I remembered, hunched over my new second-hand
Elizabeth David cookbook and then the measure

of this thought, guessing what herbs
would bring out best that particular moist
sub-rural English gamey flavour, while you

in the room's other half were watching
or not watching TV, the worked-up
bouts of laughter, little yelps and bouncy camera angles

so threading into your nerves
the doomy Big Ben toll of ITN news
came as relief, in its way: bailiffs failing again

to evict protesters, frescos in Assissi damaged
(delivered, this, with a palpable sense
of affront) by small Italian earthquake.

The twins upstairs – the one bunched up,
the other splayed to the world, postures habitual
as signatures – slept on. A car's beams swept up

and through the room, and when I came back down
to you – that, and when *We'll take a break now*,
said Trevor, *and after the break* – the afterlife,

it seemed, could be this: this sitting around, late,
watching ads for panty liners and macho cars
and worrying what's to become

of the boys and girls in the trees tonight,
maybe wafted so high
by whatever they're on, their lives

of wind and wild berries, some poisonous, some not.

Russians

They live, in general, on the fourth floor (the fourth floor of the translator, which is usually the third floor for us Italians, or French or Germans). They walk not up and down but from one corner to another.

Aldo Buzzi, *Journey to the Land of the Flies*

I was briefly a guest of the Russians
before I became a machinist, and had to move out.
I still miss my handmade boots (pity the Catholics,
living below!), and not having to shave.

From the seventh floor you can see as far as the ring road,
but we machinists had little time to enjoy the view.
Anything except work was illegal,
as the work was too.

For now I have found my level
among the *petite bourgeoisie*
who live above their shops and workshops
on the first (or, as the Americans have it, the second) floor.

We repair upholstery and sell magazines
that propagate our strange but true beliefs:
that egg yolk is good for the scalp,
that love conquers all.

On summer nights
the strains of drinking songs
drift down from above.
On winter mornings I sometimes think

that if I was not already married
I would like to marry the Cossack girl with pigtails
out foraging for fuel
for their wood-burning stoves.

Theories of the Leisure Class

*The office of the leisure class in social evolution is to retard the
movement, and to conserve what is obsolescent.*
    Thorstein Veblen, *The Theory of the Leisure Class* (1899)

That standing to attention for the national anthem never did
    us any harm.
That nor did boiled cabbage and burnt toast, despite its being
    carcinogenic.
That food wrapped in clingfilm lowers your sperm count.

That men under average height are more aggressive.
That it's something in the brake fluid that causes it.
That science can explain everything.

That what goes up must trickle down.
That we have come a long way since semiology.
That where would we be now but for the nuclear deterrent
    and the fear of God.

That we all know what married men are like.
That divorce counsellors with beards come from broken
    homes.
That sleeping with the light on makes you go blind.

That getting and spending is good for the thighs and lower
    back.
That profits from the sale under licence of the gene for
    happiness will transform the marketplace.
That the welfare state is all very well.

That in the future, we will live for ever.
That irony is a finite resource.
That looters should be shot on sight.

Summer School

Who does he think he is? – latecomers
may wonder, lovers playing truant or the odd-job man
in overalls, priming the railings pink.

The Marquis de la Mole? The health & safety inspector?
These hot afternoons
on the terrace on the Union cafeteria

I've become a fixture, a recurring motif,
sitting out the seminar on theories of comedy,
or the Romance languages, or crisis management,

and hardly bothering even to shoo off
the black ungainly birds
that teeter on table edges, making stabs at crusts ...

At five on the dot the students filter out,
blinking in the light. They stand around,
unsure of what next, impersonating mourners.

I lie back in my chair, face to the azure sky,
while the waitress gathers two coins
from under a saucer, and applies them to my eyes.

Eleanor of Aquitaine

Roses, I say, holy relics, the plaintive songs
of your favourite troubadour.

Dung, she replies. *Horse-shit. Ordure.*
We simply lack the detergents ...

Marriage negotiations are put on hold
while a posse of Crusaders goes clanking by

and the blue-eyed boys in the next-door valley
sharpen the rules of perspective.

Third Alibi (The Blessings)

Home and dry, I was counting my blessings
and then counting them again
in case I had missed one – my apparent sanity,
or the bottle of Chilean Merlot
I had only just opened.

I remember the Gothic script
on the label, I remember looking out from the kitchen
  window
at the windows of the houses opposite
and feeling, briefly,
both content and lucky, then neither at all.

I paid my dues, I read the reviews,
and when the minister spoke on TV I neither agreed
nor disagreed. I wrote a letter
to a friend who was dead, he would understand,
I thought, though at the point
when he began finishing my sentences for me
I put down my pen ...

Around midnight I went for a walk,
it had been raining earlier,
the streets were quiet, now and then a car
with headlights dipped, making good its escape.

Fourth Alibi (Room 209)

By the time I looked around
what had happened had happened
and the place was empty, just the waitress
sitting up at the bar, talking quietly
with the barman
about her overland trip to wherever.

By the time it really hit me
I was walking down Southampton Row,
stopping at each hotel
and claiming to be a resident.

In the end I just asked for 209
and was given the key. Then the lift
to the second floor, the room with its teak
veneer, its mirrors and sporting prints,
the bed I had made for myself
and a view from the rainblurred window

of factories for sale
where bats inhabit the loading bays,
telephones ring in Accounts –
ring and go dead and ring again –

and the man by the yard gate
in his ink-stained suit
is the cross-eyed boy I teased in school

with his coins and pieces of string
and his polka-dot handkerchief,
practising his magic tricks.

14th February Street

Valentine's Day, and my lips are sealed.
But I will say this: that the balloons
tethered to the railing outside a basement wine bar
advertising Happy Hour 5 to 7,
two drinks for the price of one –
that these heart-shaped helium-filled fluorescent balloons
which rise and sag, shiver and crinkle
according to the draughts of passing traffic,
according to the weather in the street,
remind me of those other ads for lump-sum investments
with small print at the bottom you're hardly meant
to read: can go down as well as up.

Street Furniture

not too sure about the springs
but in need of a breather I settle in
on a worn but not damp second-hand armchair
placed hospitably in front of what used
to be Regent Office Supplies and in fact still says so
on the board above the shop
with only the second E missing now there
's a woman I would cross the road for
and Mrs Bargolini the dinner lady
odd how you know the face before you can place it
she must think I'm being unfriendly
and the man from the halal butcher's I reckon
you could teach yourself Arabic if you sat here
long enough or at least work out what to do
about global warming or Father McMahon who's lost again
on the 3 o'clock at Kempton Park and I've opened
a beer it's hot today the brain
needs lubrication and life is short
my friends too much of it just waiting
for the queue to move the kettle to boil the paint
to dry and people vanish too soon vanish
between the bottle-bank and the Polish deli
between amber and green in a cloud of exhaust
when this man steps out from the door behind
and asks if I think this chair
was put here just for me to sit on

Long Story Short

1 *Early Days*

Pilots crash-landed. Arms were devoured
by threshing-machines. Grown men bitten by snakes
died in agony
within twenty-four hours, while children
simply vanished – she was down
by the river washing clothes, she was heating up beans
in the kitchen, she screwed up her eyes
and cupped a hand above her brows and stared
past the cemetery, past the telegraph station,
but she knew they were gone.

On the other hand, God existed.

On the other hand, she sat in the shade for years
whittling sticks
into curious knotted shapes
with mouths and ears, penises and vaginas
and other organs
I no longer recall.

2 *The Boom Years*

When he wanted to sober up
he drove to the top of Beacon Hill
with a couple of beers and his woman
and watched the money rolling in.

The lights. The glitz. The *boom-boom*
of the nightclub bass and the round-the-clock mills
and the ache in his jaw
after her husband caught them in bed.

The taste, salty and sweet,
of the patch behind her earlobe
he kept coming back to for more.

3 *The Flipper People*

Encumbered as we are –
with buckets and spades, swimwear, towels,
picnic boxes, bronzing lotions, paperback biographies
and glossy magazines in which minor royalty
reveal the secrets of their wardrobes –
we wear the flippers, it seems easier than carrying them.

Flip-flop we go across a muddy field
in perfect iambs
to the shingle beach. Flip-flop.

The sun will bake the mud hard.
Later, light falls of volcanic ash will cover
and preserve our flipper prints, so that you among others
will draw the wrong conclusions.

Casual Work

When our children try to read between the lines
of our autograph books, we tell them about the year
the angels held their convention
at the Station Hotel.

Their debates on revisionist heresies
and minimum wingspans
passed over our heads, and we failed to seduce even one,
but we carried their Samsonite briefcases.

We fixed up the overhead projector.
We replenished their bottled water.
We recommended seafood restaurants.
We aired their rooms.

Moonlighting

It's later than you think. The waiter yawns.
The cook, the under-cook, the barman, the trainee
manager who's barely out of school, all yawn.
Then the woman in the tricky blue blouse –
shamelessly, with all her heart – and the delegates
from the menswear conference who are on expenses,
with the drinks bill to prove it, the bald man
reading Dickens and the German mum-and-dad-
and-two-bored-teenagers, also the pasty man
sitting opposite the woman in blue, checking his watch.
His wife too – you'd think this yawn
would have tired itself out, would be raising one hand
to its opening mouth, but no – his wife at home
in the bedroom doorway, her weight against the jamb,
watching their only child asleep. The doorman
downstairs, the conductor on the night bus
passing by, even the Pope, on the TV behind the bar,
is yawning, 2000 years of Christianity and still
they don't get it, Europe, the Western world
baring its wet pink gums
and livid tongue, as if slowly beginning
to turn itself inside out ...
                    While I, in a borrowed apron
behind the swing-doors, scrape half a raspberry pavlova
into the bin and plunge the plate
into scummy water (a white-collar man by day,
I am seized at times by an urgent need
to do something manual, something involving dirt).

West One

Who owns these women with perfect skin
in low-cut T-shirts, who leaves them sitting around
all morning in cafés?
                              So finely made
and with such care, such loving attention to detail,
then left to make their way
in this giddy world – as she now arriving late,
very late, but so pleased
with her new pretty things in tissue-wrap
and spangled bags my endorphins can't help
but get going, slippy little fellas
riding their luck –
                              And I do too
like the way they stride off
with their arms clasped tight across their breasts
as if the weather had suddenly changed.

Meanwhile the helplines are jammed, my soufflés
fail to rise, my anger and depressions ...

My Overthrow

Bandits from the hills infiltrated the town.
They sold blood-red roses at busy intersections,
whispering through the windows of rush-hour traffic
sublime promises, subversive rumours. They loitered
in stairwells, telling jokes with slow-burning punchlines.
They trained stray dogs to follow me to work
and stand by my office door, whimpering softly.
They handed out fliers for public executions.
They hummed continuous loops of martial music.
They forged my signature and ordered in my name
high-quality luxury goods: an electric wheelchair,
a commemorative dinner service, a shredding machine
into which I fed the instruction manual and three-year
guarantee and – in error, in my eagerness to please –
my life-savings certificates. They played football
on the palace lawn and deliberately kicked the ball
into the path of my car, forcing me to swerve violently
and run over a cat – its eyes softened
in recognition, its entrails were spotted with black.

I got home late. On the mantelpiece,
a single rose, every petal intact. I took off my clothes
and folded them neatly, how I'd folded them for years:
lean years and fat, fallow, madcap, *démodé* years
of unclassifiable material, half eaten by moths,
swaying when I breathed, with the indelible smell of me.

PART THREE

An Aberration

Something about, something to do with ...
Hard to recall just now

quite what we were speaking of
before that couple of show-off police cars

and a stark raving ambulance
came blaring by, drowning us out,

carving a bully-boy path
through the meek mid-morning traffic –

and not entirely blameless too
the man with the cardiac arrest

or the child who climbed over a fence
and got a high electric dose

or the woman whose contractions came on
so suddenly, *ambushed* her really,

catching her unawares – something
about, something to do with the shape

of your neck ...

The Pink Hotel

We renamed the streets after our favourite songs
and sat on the sun-deck of the Pink Hotel
watching drivers get first confused, then angry,
then tearing their maps into bite-sized pieces.

A waiter frisked us for prohibited substances.
Small children approached in ones and twos
and shyly asked who wrote the lyrics
of the road to the cottage hospital.

It dawned upon us we were running late,
and as we hurried along to the artist's studio
the children began repainting the hotel
in greens and browns, a precautionary measure.

We posed naked for statues of ourselves.
We woke late, lifelike but blanketed by snow
on which a most delicate crust
had formed overnight.

Skadarlija

This was the café I'd go to
when I couldn't stand being in the same house as the person
or persons I'd just quarrelled with
and the temperature was below freezing
and I'd left my lighter in the pocket of my other jacket.
Fortunately there were heavy smokers there
from whom I could bum a light
and then another, as I sat at the counter by the window
nursing my hot cup of self-righteousness
and looking out at the snow drifting down but not settling,
as it rarely does in cities, sudden flurries or eddies
and the people so intent and wrapped up
they might have been sleepwalking. I could sit here
happily, I remember thinking – while the men around me
who greeted one another like brothers, as if they'd all grown up
in one household, one rambling overpopulated villa
down an unpaved lane, students and refugees and local
entrepreneurs, chess-playing grandfathers and always at least
one beautiful woman, talked in their language
and ignored me – I could sit here happily
for the rest of my life; but it may be I was only waiting
for the flower-seller to come in through the door
with his bunches of ready-wrapped roses, tulips even,
which to last a little longer
should be cut diagonally and crushed across the stem
before they are placed in water.

Cabin Fever

Abandoning the aircraft: Open cockpit door. Disconnect
intercommunication lead and undo safety harness. Slide over the
side, head foremost and facing the tail.
            Pilot's Notes for Tiger Moth Aircraft (RAAF, 1944)

A buzz in the air, in her head, disturbing
what was hardly a train of thought.
Something to be fixed, attended to . . .

He comes in low, skimming the trees
from which shrill black birds rise up in alarm
as the engine coughs, stutters, then gives up the ghost.

                    *

It's to do with age, she thinks, with obsolescence.
She's standing in this little hut
by the runway, not touching anything –
oil-drums, tools, trays of bolts and wing-nuts,
old grease-stained maps and manuals,
two unwashed mugs, a stack of magazines
dating, she just knows, from the early fifties:
a place a man might now and then
step into, take what he wants
and leave, not forgetting to lock the door.

                    *

At the governor's reception
he stands stock still, rooted
to the parquet floor, balancing his glass of cloudy wine
and his plate of tidbits, on the one hand innocence,

on the other experience, while the breasts
of jasmine-scented women brush lightly by him
and the governor's ten-year-old daughter
runs in circles with arms outstretched,
making aeroplane noises.

*

Once, he tells her, setting the oil-can
back on the shelf, wiping the grease off his hands,
he flew to America. He was driven by limousine
into Manhattan. He had just sat down
in the fourth-floor lounge
of his budget hotel, a bourbon in his hand,
when a suicide fell past the window.

Or the time the ailerons jammed with ice
at 11,000 feet, and when he hit a spot of turbulence
the whole thing skewed, bucked
and went into a corkscrew dive, spinning,
unravelling, until, falling through
beneath the clouds, no more than 50 feet above the waves,
he opened the throttle and levelled out.

*

The people of the Celebes opened their hearts:
the runway was garnished with pale blue flowers.
The people of Chiang Mai were nervous
and those of Dakar, generous to a fault.
Of Denver, depressed. Of Kandahar
and also Wuzhou, ambidextrous. In Vientiane
the streets were deserted, it was a holiday
for the dead, even the dead
need a change of air, a time to unwind.

This morning the sky is overcast
and they're doing some routine maintenance:
tightening the rigging,
adjusting the rudder pedals.

She walks towards him, scratching her left upper arm.
He is wiping his hands on a rag.

Afterwards, after the ground crew have dispersed
and enough time has elapsed
for her to remove her glasses
and change into a light summer frock
that leaves her shoulders bare,
he plans to tell her the truth.

*

She's been closing her eyes, she's been landing
in a mellow dune
close by a watering hole
where zebras congregate at dusk –

she can hear them drinking, sucking rather,
until the daylight has utterly gone
and the white of their stripes –

she's been telling herself
life doesn't happen like this
except sometimes, which is why
the emergency services seem under-rehearsed.

Unexamined Life

A fine dust drifts down from the sky,
visible only against dark walls, dark foliage.

Did I remember to cancel the newspaper?
To lock the back door? To wipe off the blood?

The exchange rate alters fractionally.
The telephone flexes its death wish.

Events with Parked Cars

The car of a beautiful woman is decorated with ribbons.
The car of someone hated, such as a tax collector:
the seats, the steering wheel, the crumpled
cigarette packets, everything is removed from the inside
and replaced by a dog. Frost sparkles
on the windscreens of several hundred parked cars
in winter sunshine as I wander among them,
trying the doors, leaving on the driver's seat
of every one that opens a handful of chopped nuts.
Parked cars are not greedy, not devious, not ironic,
unless the handbrake is off. Some are occupied
by unshaven single men in their forties or fifties,
they sit hunched in silent pools of sorrow, anger
and sullen pride in having no home to go home to.
Once as a child I watched a car being lifted
onto a flat-bed truck and taken away to a distant compound,
my secret wishes still clamped beneath its wipers.
My uncle had this talent: he would fiddle around
beneath a parked car and emerge with a pail of milk.
Brides on Saturdays make commanding gestures –
halt! move left! – while women hang pots and pans,
ladles and nylon brushes from the aerials of parked cars
and the men read newspapers. To scatter an enemy
across the outlying districts, scratch his name
with a coin on the bonnets of adjacent parked cars.
The car of an adulterer is painted yellow.
The car of a sailor always lists to one side.
For making love in, a car should be parked off the road
in pouring rain. A decent mechanic can tell your fortune

from the rust on the chassis, that crusty bronze.
Traffic cones obstructing a parking space
signify a recent death. As the dead exceed
the living, so do parked cars those in motion.
Over one car and then the next and then the next
I make my way to the river, never touching the ground.

The Wellington Group

*The term refers to a loose association of New Zealand poets in
Wellington, in the years between 1950 and 1965 ... Certainly James
K. Baxter and Louis Johnson, both Wellington residents during
the period, seemed to draw a number of poets around them: Alastair
Campbell, for example, and the immigrants Peter Bland and
Charles Boyle.*

      The Oxford Companion to Twentieth-Century Poetry

Remind me, Peter,

what was on the agenda – weren't we trying to prove a point
to the eggheads up in Auckland

about truth to experience, the sacredness
of where and when and who?

Since I returned to London in nineteen-whatever
to start all over, to write my *bildungsroman*

of a wild colonial boy
in the new Elizabethan age, I seem to have lost touch

almost with my own life: my children look at me
as if across a genetic barrier,

and did I really sleep with Miss South Island
'63, or was that something else

I made up for the c.v.? But sometimes, Peter,
after lunch with my agent

in a restaurant where not even the cloakroom attendant
pretends he knows me, I'm there again –

among the bottles and books and rhyming voices
in a draughty upstairs room

where James K. Baxter holds me on his knee.
I am four years old. I don't want to go to bed.

Literals

On the north side,
where it catches the sun in the morning,
the horse in which Henry James was born.

No frisky palomino,
its flanks slowly swell and subside
with deep convoluted breaths.

Critics, bailiffs, and sellers of life assurance
are summarily dismissed
by a lazy flick of its tail.

Thirty seconds before we go out live –
small talk in the hospitality room,
the make-up assistant powdering my balls,

then drawing her comb
one final time
through my public hair – I get this criminal urge

to *épater les bourgeois*,
to expose myself to the nation
in collar and tie, trousers, socks, the full attire.

Ask them why so sad,
the streets-weepers here
in the dun garb of the borough cleansing department,

and they look at you
with red and swollen eyes
as if you alone had failed to notice

how early it gets dark,
and that the Seas of Tranquillity and Ingenuity
are dry as a bone.

The Body Double

Also that look
you give me, as if I was someone famous
you'd chanced upon in Tesco,

but somehow less tall, young, sexy or dead
than you'd supposed, maybe even
not me after all, not the one, say,

in *The English Patient*
who carries Kristin Scott Thomas
out of the cave, but the one in the ad

for Renault cars, or was it Ford.

The Lady with the Dog

*One evening I was sitting on the bridge which is at the bottom of
Richmond Terrace, reading Mrs Hutchinson's Memoirs – one of my
passions. 'Mister Bell!' a man said, stopping right in front of me.*
                                    Stendhal, *Souvenirs d'Egotisme*

I heard my name, or almost my name, called across the street
– 'Beyle!' – and made the mistake of turning round. A whistle
blew, the traffic stopped, a woman with a yapping dog in tow
bustled across and kissed me on both cheeks. She was mis-
taken, I told her. No, she insisted upon it, she knew my
teasing ways, I was Beyle, Henry Beyle, also known as
Stendhal, also known as Charlier, Aubertin, Bliarce, Louis-
César-Alexandre Bombet, Octavien-Henri Fairmontfort,
Dominique, Darlincourt, Ceranuto, Leimery, l'Animal,
d'Averny, Le Bourlier, oh, she could go on, did I know that
the critics studying my correspondence had discovered some
350 aliases in addition? No wonder she was confused, I said,
disentangling my leg from the forepaws of the dog, and
besides, who was she? George Sand? She blushed. The dog
stood off. For a moment I wondered if I had, in fact, met this
woman before. Did I owe her money? An apology? Had I
caused offence? (Beyle, I knew, though not a handsome man,
was not without whatever it is to which women respond with
that mixture of lust and entrepreneurial spirit that keeps the
show on the road, and so often leads to tears.) A moment, as I
said – but the dog, sensing indecision, slipped its collar and
scampered away towards King's Cross. It was one of those
literary dogs that feature in quizzes in the books pages of
Sunday papers at Christmas time.

The Privileges

(after Stendhal)

Arriving in small towns where both hotels are full,
may I find that a room in the prettier one
has unexpectedly become available.
May this room have a balcony, a bed with a firm mattress,
a selection of my favourite books from thirty years ago
and a telephone that will bring me the voice
of a former lover, now resident in this town
with a rich, complaisant husband and a fondness
for shellfish, basil, garlic and Parmesan.

*

At home or abroad, may I be able to converse
fluently and with the correct accent in the language
of whomever I am addressing. Such fluency
in foreign tongues to be extended to the writing of letters,
but not to any work intended for publication.

*

May I be permitted to park on double yellow lines
without penalty, to pay no income tax
and to write one decent poem every six weeks.
May my bowel movements, waterworks and sexual
competence remain untrammelled by age or disease.

*

Every so often may I get off my arse
and join in the game in the park and surprise myself
by performing some feat of unparalleled natural-born skill

which the others will take for granted.
May children entrust to me
astounding secrets which I will never betray.

＊

Three times a year may I sleep past my stop on the tube
and become, for as long as it amuses me, a woman.
Midwinter weekday mornings, a love letter would be nice:
a real one, something I have to live up to. And besides
all that – remembering six good jokes and never losing my keys
or having to queue – may I be continually surprised
by whatever happens next.

From the Rooftops

Dress up your roofs! Think of them as hairdos, add some pretty pins.

Velimir Khlebnikov

For answering back, for wanting more
than you can have, you are sent to your room
with no supper. The moon
shines biddingly, you climb through the open hatch
onto the roof: neglected, bare, superior
waste ground, with space and to spare
for your bed, bedside table and collection of shells.

Here you spend your adolescence
looking down the cleavages
of passing women, while at regular intervals
your parents float by on a cloud,
still bickering or reading their books
with the difficult words that spill down the page
in an orderly queue, as if waiting for permission
to turn over, then turning
over all the same ... And one evening
in late June, a bright and windless day, on a roof
just fourteen paces across, distracted perhaps
by a man with a monocle
who is jotting something down in his notebook –
some witty aperçu, some off-the-cuff sketch
of yourself against the skyline –
you take fifteen steps
and fly, a little clumsily at first,
over to Marine Ices for a triple scoop.

Then back out west
to the Bush, showing off to your friends your new
life skill, climbing the thermal risers
and hovering in perfect balance
before the sudden plunge and swoop –
like signing a cheque for a million,
like the brushstrokes of a Chinese master
in ink on rice paper, that tight reverse flick
as if practised for years – away
over Acton and Ealing, streets and back gardens,
lock-ups, repair shops, a bicycle front wheel
chained to the railings, a bentwood chair
left out all winter, other lost
civilisations, before settling exhausted to roost
under the eaves of a disused chapel,
now a discount carpet warehouse.

Here a dream kicks in
of an ancient oak, its scribble of roots
tapering down
through the mulch and dark, until the gate's unlocked
for an early delivery
and an elderly yard-man struggles by hand
with rolls of carpet twice his height
because the fork-lift truck is broken.
Life is hard, is the gist of what he is muttering
under his breath, each day is filled
with many obstacles to surmount. But you,
you have the means to do this.

Summer, an Afternoon

Summer, an afternoon, with time to kill,
I enter the bar behind the abbey
and there by the window is my love
at a table for two, writing postcards.

She has been busy (I am reading
over her shoulder, I am nibbling
her salted almonds, I am licking her stamps
with the portrait of Henry the Navigator).

She has bought a leather coat
and cannot imagine when she will wear it.
She has been to the art gallery
three times, and in that rushed, familiar hand
she wonders why it is
she is so drawn to paintings that are dark, and late,
and to which the photos on the reverse fail to do justice.

I reach across to offer her a light.
She misses everyone ...
I reach across to offer her a light

or share her wine or touch
her cheek or add my bit along the bottom edge
or in the margin, but this poem
is closing now, the waiters
are checking their watches, the abbey
is being rolled up, oxygen levels are critical

as we leave hurriedly through a small back room
containing crates of empty bottles,
knives, a mirror, a cat curled like an ammonite
on a three-legged chair.

Notes and Asides

Follain's Leeds 'He has spoken with a shudder of the possibility of having been born even a year or so later (his birth date was August 29, 1903) and so not being able to remember the whole existence that, as he testified, vanished with the 1914–1918 war. And when, in 1919, he was sent to England (Leeds) to learn the language, his resistance to the enterprise took the form of a refusal to believe that there was more than one way of naming a thing.' Translator's introduction to *Transparence of the World*, poems by Jean Follain selected and translated by W. S. Merwin, New York, 1969.

The Wellington Group For Charles Boyle, I'm told by Peter Bland, read Charles Doyle (who moved to Canada in the 1960s).

Literals 'Whenever I come across a misprint, I think something new has been invented' – Goethe (quoted by D. J. Enright). 1: 'I pass on to the row of horses on the north side of the square. Henry James was born in one of these … they are plainly old, though no longer aristocratic: haughty last-century shabbies with shut eyelids …' – Cynthia Ozick, 'Washington Square, 1946', in *Portrait of the Artist as a Bad Character*, London, 1996. 2: '… Fiona, who was a very over-developed girl with heavy breasts and startlingly thick public hair, stiff and proud and rust-coloured, like dead bracken' – Cressida Connolly, 'The Pleasure Gardens', in *London Magazine*, June/July 1999. 3: the streets-weepers are from a *Sunday Times* colour magazine article in the 1980s.

[78]

From the Rooftops Khlebnikov, writing in around 1917, continues: 'People will no longer gather in the vicious streets, whose dirty desire reduces human beings to residue in a washbasin; rather they will throng upon the rooftops, beautiful young rooftops, waving their handkerchiefs after a giant levitating air-cloud, sending goodbyes and farewells after their departing friends' (*The King of Time: Selected Writing of the Russian Futurian*, translated by Paul Schmidt, edited by Charlotte Douglas, Cambridge, Mass., and London, 1985). The man with the monocle is Anton Chekhov: 'He drove in a cab, and, as he watched his son walking away, thought: Perhaps he belongs to the race of men who will no longer trundle in scurvy cabs, as I do, but will fly through the skies in balloons' (*Notebook*, translated by S. S. Koteliansky and Leonard Woolf, New York, 1921). Also to the point is Vilém Flusser (in *The Shape of Things*, London, 1999): 'Roofs are devices to make us subservient.'